Damsel Producti
Theatre   μ. esents

THE AMBER TRAP

by Tabitha Mortiboy

‖ SAMUEL FRENCH ‖

samuelfrench.co.uk

DAMSEL
PRODUCTIONS

The Amber Trap premiered at Theatre503, London on 24 April 2019 with the following cast (in alphabetical order) and creatives:

HOPE	Fanta Barrie
JO	Jenny Bolt
MICHAEL	Misha Butler
KATIE	Olivia Rose Smith

Director	Hannah Hauer-King
Producer	Kitty Wordsworth
Designer	Jasmine Swan
Lighting Designer	Lucy Adams
Sound Designer	Annie May Fletcher

Production Manager	Zara Janmohamed
Stage Manager	Katie Bachtler
Associate Producer	George Jaques
Assistant Director	Anastasia Bruce-Jones
Assistant Producer	Katie Paterson
Assistant Stage Manager	Kat Wellman
Assistant Production Manager	Emma Dobson
Fight Director	Enric Ortuño

CAST

Fanta Barrie – HOPE

Fanta is a graduate of Rose Bruford College.

Since graduating, her stage credits include: *Songlines* (HighTide Festival / Edinburgh Fringe) and *The Cereal Cafe* (The Other Palace Theatre).

Jenny Bolt – JO

Jenny studied at Dartington College of Arts.

Her stage credits include: *Dusty* (UK Tour); *Electra* (Old Vic); *A Long Way From Home* (Tricycle); *Dark Tourism and The Last Room I Checked* (Arcola); *Sleeping Beauty* (City Varieties Leeds); *Soiled Stock* and *A Boutique Hotel in Battersea* (Landor Theatre).

On screen, Jenny has appeared in *Call The Midwife* (BBC); *Casualty* (BBC); *London's Burning* (LWT); *Holby City* (BBC); *Hollyoaks* (C4); *Dream Team* (Sky); *The Bill* (ITV); *Coronation Street* (ITV); *Emmerdale* (ITV); *Staying Alive* (LWT); *Cherished* (ITV) and *Parents' Night* (C4).

Jenny is also a stand-up comedian and acting tutor/teacher.

Misha Butler – MICHAEL

Misha is nineteen and grew up in London.

His TV credits include: *Casualty* and *Doctors*. He played a leading role in the highly-acclaimed Netflix/Channel4 series, *Kiss me First*. A successful tour of *The Winslow Boy* marked his professional stage debut, followed by *Jess and Joe Forever* at The Stephen Joseph. This is Misha's first time performing at Theatre503.

Olivia Rose Smith – KATIE

Olivia is a graduate of the Oxford School of Drama.

Television credits include: *Scott & Bailey* Series 2-4 (ITV) and *Moving On* Series 4 & 6 (BBC).

Theatre whilst training includes: *Conditionally*; *Tiger Country*; *Love's Labour's Lost*; *Fear and Misery of the Third Reich*; *The Comedy of Errors*; *Machinal* and *Man of Mode*.

CREATIVES

Hannah Hauer-King – Director

Hannah is a London based theatre director, and Artistic Director and co-founder of Damsel Productions. After moving from the US, she started her London directing career acting as Resident AD at Soho Theatre in 2014. She now works as a freelance theatre director, and has worked at venues including Southwark Playhouse, Soho Theatre, Traverse Theatre and Bunker Theatre. She also works as a script reader for the NT, as well as a theatre, comedy and cabaret programmer for Live At Zedel.

Most recent directing work includes: *The Funeral Director* (Southwark Playhouse & UK Tour 2019); *Fabric* (Soho Theatre); *Grotty* (Bunker Theatre); *Fury* (Soho Theatre); *The Swell* (Hightide Festival); *Breathe* (Bunker Theatre); *Revolt She Said Revolt Again* (RCSSD); *Clay* (Pleasance Theatre); *Witt 'n Camp* (Edinburgh Fringe, Assembly); *Dry Land* (Jermyn Street Theatre). Associate/Assistant work: *Romeo & Juliet* (Shakespeare's Globe), *Radiant Vermin* (Soho Theatre) and *Daytona* (Theatre Royal Haymarket).

Kitty Wordsworth – Producer

Kitty Wordsworth is a freelance theatre, comedy and screen producer. She is executive producer and co-founder of Damsel Productions. She also works part-time at West End production company, Lee Menzies Ltd, in the marketing team at Ronnie Scott's, and with arts events and fundraising specialist company, Act IV. After graduating from Sussex University in 2014, she produced the Portobello Pantomime, *Peter Panto* (Tabernacle, December 2014).

Recent theatre producer credits include: *Fabric* (Soho Theatre and London Tour); *Grotty* (The Bunker); *Damsel Develops* (The Bunker); *Fury* (Soho Theatre); *Dry Land* (Jermyn Street Theatre); *Uncensored* (Theatre Royal Haymarket); *TABS* (workshop, Tristan Bates Theatre); *Snow White and the Seven Runaways* (Tabernacle); *The Naivety: A Journey* (Tabernacle); *Dick Whit* (Tabernacle); *The Snow Queen* (Tabernacle); *Brute* (Soho Theatre) and *Juliet Cowan: Eat, Pray, Call the Police* (Live @Zedel). Associate theatre producer credits include: *A Level Playing Field* (Jermyn Street Theatre) and *Ever HopeFull* (So and So Arts Club).

Film producer credits include: *Little Hard* (dir. Bel Powley and Alice Felgate); *The Last Birthday* (dir. Jaclyn Bethany); *Sunday* (dir. Daisy Stenham); *Once Upon a Time's Up* (dir. Denna Cartamkhoob) and *Conditionally* (in development).

Jasmine Swan - Designer

Theatre work includes: *Armadillo* (The Yard); *Sonny* (Arts Educational Schools); *The Tide Jetty* (Eastern Angles Touring Theatre Company); *Eden* (Hampstead Theatre); *Sex Sex Men Men* (The Yard); Chutney (The Bunker) *Off West End Nominated for Best Set Design*; *Lost Boys New Town* (National Youth Theatre); *Women in Power* (Nuffield Southampton Theatres & Oxford Playhouse); *Medusa* (NST Studio); *Son Of Rambow* (The Other Palace); *Much Ado About Nothing, Dungeness, Love & Information* (Nuffield Southampton Youth Theatre); *Sleuth* (ZoieLogic Dance Theatre); *Cabaret* (Westminster School); *Hanna* (Regional Tour starting at The Arcola, Papatango); *The Passing of the Third Floor Back* (Finborough Theatre); *Hyem* (Theatre503 & Northern Stage); *Who's Afraid Of The Working Class?* (Unity Theatre) and *The Wonderful World of Dissocia* (Liverpool Playhouse Studio).

Jasmine was a finalist in the Linbury Prize for Stage Design 2017 and was multiple nominated for Best Designer in The Stage Debut Awards 2018, for her designs at: Theatre503, Finborough Theatre and The Arcola. She was the Laboratory Associate Designer for Nuffield Southampton Theatres 2017/18. Jasmine trained at Liverpool Institute for Performing Arts, where she also received the Ede & Ravenscroft Prize for Creative and Technical Excellence (2016). www.jasmineswan.com

Lucy Adams - Lighting Designer

Lucy Adams is a London based lighting designer working in devised work and new writing. She's an associate artist with ThisEgg, having designed *Goggles, Me and My Bee, UNCONDITIONAL* and *dressed.* (Fringe First Award winner) for the company. She's also worked with BREACH Theatre on *It's True, It's True, It's True* (Fringe First Award winner); Barrel Organ on *Anyone's Guess How We Got Here*; YESYESNONO on *[insert slogan here]*; Willy Hudson on *Bottom* (Edinburgh Fringe and Soho Theatre);

and Haley McGee on *Ex-Boyfriend Yard Sale* (Camden People's Theatre). Her lighting design for new writing includes: *Skin A Cat* by Isley Lynn directed by Blythe Stewart (UK tour); *One Jewish Boy* by Stephen Laughton directed by Sarah Meadows (Old Red Lion) and *A Hundred Words for Snow* by Tatty Hennessy directed by Lucy Atkinson (Vault Festival and Trafalgar Studios).

Annie May Fletcher - Sound Designer

Annie is a freelance sound designer and composer for theatre based in London and West Yorkshire. She graduated from LAMDA's Technical Theatre & Stage Management Fda course and she is currently Laboratory Associate Sound Designer at Nuffield Southampton Theatres 2018/19. Annie is also an Associate Artist with Snapper Theatre, a female-led new writing company who she has collaborated with on *Thomas* (The Vaults) and *Lobster* (Theatre503).

Her other recent sound designs include: *How To Disappear Completely And Never Be Found* and *Humbug! The Hedgehog Who Couldn't Sleep* at Nuffield Southampton Theatres; *3 Billion Seconds*, *Vespertilio* and *Alcatraz* (The Vaults); *Ad Libido* (Soho Theatre, The Vaults); *Weird* (Pleasance); *Filth* (theSpace); *Chatroom* and *Burn* (Tristan Bates); *Broken* (Old Red Lion) and *Moonfleece* (Pleasance). www.anniemayfletcher.co.uk

Katie Bachtler - Stage Manager

Theatre as Company Stage Manager/Stage Manager on Book includes: *The Hoes* (Hampstead Theatre Downstairs); *soft animals* (Soho Theatre); *Fabric* (Damsel Productions, Soho Theatre); *Big Aftermath of a Small Disclosure* (ATC, Summerhall, Edinburgh Fringe); *A New and Better You* (The Yard, London); *Grotty* (Damsel Productions, The Bunker); *Winter Solstice* (ATC, UK Tour); *Dear Brutus* (Southwark Playhouse, London) and Assembly Festival at the Edinburgh Fringe as Technical Stage Manager. Events include: Gibson Street Gala, Kentish Town Community Festival, and the annual Glasgow Film Festival as Venue Coordinator. Trained at Edinburgh Stage Management School, and completed an MA in English Literature and Theatre Studies at the University of Glasgow.

| Press Representation | Kate Morley PR |
| Marketing Consultant | Kalle Jurvanen for Target Live |

Poster Photography	Daisy Dalton
Production Photography	The Other Richard
Other Photography	George Jaques
Graphic Design	Baker, Fionn O'Neill, Conor Jatter

Special thanks to: Arts Council England, Adwoa Aboah, Bryony Coleman, Casa Tua Camden, Cassie Beadle, Christopher D Clegg, Claudia Paterson, Cob Gallery, Debra Hauer, Ekaterina Kashyntseva, ETT, Florence Huntinton-Whiteley, Fork Deli Patisserie, Hampstead Theatre, James Campbell, James Jaques, Jerwood Space, Kam Nagpal, Lemon & Limes, Nike, Nutty Williams, Opera Holland Park, Reuben Hamlyn, Shodirb Rehamn from Merchant Street Costcutter, Target Live, the Young Vic and 3B Scientific.

SUBSIDISED REHEARSAL FACILITIES PROVIDED BY

JERWOOD SPACE

This production has been licensed by arrangement with The Agency (London) Ltd, 24 Pottery Lane, London, W11 4LZ. Email: info@theagency.co.uk.

Hannah Hauer-King and Kitty Wordsworth co-founded Damsel Productions in 2015 to place women's voices centre stage. Damsel Productions hopes to be one cog in a larger and crucial movement addressing both the misrepresentation and under-representation of women in theatre. The idea is simple: to bring together women directors, producers, designers and all other creatives to breathe life into scripts exclusively written by women. Damsel Productions aim to provoke, inspire and entertain with true and honest representations of the female experience.

Critically successful productions include the UK première of Ruby Rae Spiegel's *Dry Land* (Jermyn Street Theatre); Izzy Tennyson's *Brute* (Soho Theatre); Phoebe Eclair-Powell's *Fury* (Soho Theatre); Izzy Tennyson's *Grotty* (The Bunker) and Abi Zakarian's *Fabric* (Soho Theatre and London community centre Tour). Damsel also recently produced London's first ever all women directing festival Damsel Develops at The Bunker.

@DamselProd
damselproductions.co.uk

Artistic Director   Hannah Hauer-King
Executive Producer   Kitty Wordsworth

Theatre503 is the home of new writers and a launchpad for the artists who bring their words to life. We are pioneers in supporting new writers and a champion of their role in the theatre ecology. We find exceptional playwrights who will define the canon for the next generation. Learning and career development are at the core of what we do. We stage the work of more debut and emerging writers than any other theatre in the country. In the last year alone we staged over 60 productions featuring 133 writers from short plays to full runs of superb drama and launching over 1,000 artists in the process. We passionately believe the most important element in a writer's development is to see their work developed through to a full production on stage, performed to the highest professional standard in front of an audience.

Over the last decade many first-time writers have gone on to establish a career in the industry thanks to the support of Theatre503: Tom Morton-Smith (*Oppenheimer*, RSC & West End), Anna Jordan (Bruntwood Prize Winner for *Yen*, Royal Exchange, Royal Court and Broadway), Vinay Patel (writer of the BAFTA winning *Murdered By My Father*), Katori Hall (*Mountaintop*, 503, West End & Broadway – winner of 503's first Olivier Award) and Jon Brittain (*Rotterdam* – winner of our second Olivier Award in 2017).

Theatre503 Team

Artistic Director	Lisa Spirling
Executive Director	Andrew Shepherd
Producer	Jake Orr
Literary Manager	Steve Harper
General Manager	Anna De Freitas
Marketing Coordinator	Jennifer Oliver
Technical Manager	Alastair Borland
Literary Associate	Lauretta Barrow
Operations Assistant	Nyanna Bentham-Prince
Resident Assistant Producers	Natalie Chan and Adam Line
Intern	Katarina Grabowsky

Theatre503 Board

Erica Whyman OBE (Chair)
Royce Bell (Vice Chair)
Chris Campbell

Joachim Fleury
Celine Gagnon
Eleanor Lloyd
Marcus Markou
Geraldine Sharpe-Newton
Jack Tilbury
Roy Williams OBE

Theatre503 Volunteers
Kelly Agredo, Emma Anderson, Elisabth Barbay, Hannah Bates, Emily Brearley-Bayliss, Alex Brent, Théo Buvat, Harley Cameron-Furze, Georgia Cusworth, Debra Dempster, Imogen Dobie, Uju Enendu, Rachel Gemaehling, Ashley Jones, Gareth Jones, Sian Legg, Andri Leonido, George Linfield, Ceri Lothian, Graham McCulloch, Ellen McGahey, Georgia McKnight, Tom Mellors, Annabel Pemberton, Lucy Robso, Kate Roche, Hannah Sands, Sussan Sanii, Kamilah Shorey, Ellie Snow, Paul Sockett, Caroline Summers Ayaaz Tariq, Thanos Topouzis, Melisa Tehrani, Camilla Walters, Stephanie Withers.

OUR SUPPORTERS

We are particularly grateful to Philip and Christine Carne and the long term support of The Carne Trust for our Playwriting Award and 503Five.

Share The Drama Patrons: Angela Hyde-Courtney, Eilene Davidson, Cas & Philip Donald, David Baxter, Erica Whyman, Geraldine Sharpe-Newton, James Bell, Jill Segal, Joakim Fleury, Nick Hern, Marcus Markou, Mike Morfey, Pam Alexander, Patricia Hamzahee, Robert O'Dowd, Roger Booker, Richard Bean, Rotha Bell, Sean Winnett.

Theatre Refurbishment: Jack Tilbury, Plann, Dynamis, CharcoalBlue, Stage Solutions, Will Bowen, The Theatres Trust

The Foyle Foundation, Arts Council England Grants for the Arts, The Peter Wolff Foundation (503 Production Fund), The Orseis Trust (503Five), Battersea Power Station Foundation (Right to Write) Barbara Broccoli/EON, Wimbledon Community Foundation (Five-O-Fresh), Nick Hern Books (503 Playwriting Award), Wandsworth Borough Council.

Theatre503 is in receipt of funding from Arts Council England's Catalyst: Evolve fund, match funding every pound raised in new income until July 2019: Evolve fund, match funding every pound raised in new income until July 2019.

THINKING ABOUT PERFORMING A SHOW?

There are thousands of plays and musicals available to perform from Samuel French right now, and applying for a licence is easier and more affordable than you might think

From classic plays to brand new musicals, from monologues to epic dramas, there are shows for everyone.

Plays and musicals are protected by copyright law, so if you want to perform them, the first thing you'll need is a licence. This simple process helps support the playwright by ensuring they get paid for their work and means that you'll have the documents you need to stage the show in public.

Not all our shows are available to perform all the time, so it's important to check and apply for a licence before you start rehearsals or commit to doing the show.

LEARN MORE & FIND THOUSANDS OF SHOWS

Browse our full range of plays and musicals, and find out more about how to license a show

www.samuelfrench.co.uk/perform

Talk to the friendly experts in our Licensing team for advice on choosing a show and help with licensing

plays@samuelfrench.co.uk   020 7387 9373

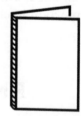

MUSIC USE NOTE

Licensees are solely responsible for obtaining formal written permission from copyright owners to use copyrighted music in the performance of this play and are strongly cautioned to do so. If no such permission is obtained by the licensee, then the licensee must use only original music that the licensee owns and controls. Licensees are solely responsible and liable for all music clearances and shall indemnify the copyright owners of the play(s) and their licensing agent, Samuel French, against any costs, expenses, losses and liabilities arising from the use of music by licensees. Please contact the appropriate music licensing authority in your territory for the rights to any incidental music.

USE OF COPYRIGHT MUSIC

A licence issued by Samuel French Ltd to perform this play does not include permission to use the incidental music specified in this copy.

Where the place of performance is already licensed by the PERFORMING RIGHT SOCIETY (PRS) a return of the music used must be made to them. If the place of performance is not so licensed then application should be made to the PRS, 2 Pancras Square, London, N1C 4AG.

A separate and additional licence from PHONOGRAPHIC PERFORMANCE LTD, 1 Upper James Street, London W1F 9DE (www.ppluk.com) is needed whenever commercial recordings are used.

IMPORTANT BILLING AND CREDIT REQUIREMENTS

If you have obtained performance rights to this title, please refer to your licensing agreement for important billing and credit requirements.

ABOUT THE AUTHOR

Tabitha Mortiboy is a playwright from London. She began her writing career in Bristol, where her first play, *Billy Through the Window*, premiered at The Wardrobe Theatre in 2015. *Billy* later transferred to Theatre 503 and to Underbelly at the Edinburgh Fringe, where it was shortlisted for the Brighton Fringe Excellence Award. In 2016 her second play, *Beacons*, was produced at the Park Theatre, London. *Beacons* was nominated for three Off West End Awards including Best New Play and Most Promising New Playwright. In 2017, she co-wrote *Bare Skin on Briny Waters* with Maureen Lennon for the Edinburgh Fringe, where it received a commendation for writing in the NSDF Edinburgh Award. As well as creating her own work, she writes alongside Bellow Theatre, a company she co-founded in 2013.e

AUTHOR'S NOTE

/	indicates an interruption
...	indicates a beat or hesitation
–	indicates a fractional pause as a word is found
( )	indicates words which may not be spoken aloud

CHARACTERS

JO – mid 50s
KATIE – early 20s
HOPE – early 20s
MICHAEL – 18

THANK YOUS

Thanks to the women of Attic Theatre who trusted me to write my first play, and who gave me the courage to write many more. Thanks especially to Jenny Lee and Louise Hill, who guided me through my first steps in the world of professional playwriting. Thanks to the women at Damsel Productions, for having faith in this story from its conception. Thanks especially to Hannah Hauer-King for her indomitable talent, precision and energy, and for being such a wonderful collaborator and dramaturg, and to Kitty Wordsworth for working tirelessly behind the scenes to turn a dream into a reality. Thanks to B.B. for a lifetime of friendship and to my family for their endless love and support. Thanks also to my agent, Jonathan, for giving me confidence and guidance on my journey as a writer. Finally, a huge, heartfelt thank you to the beautiful and brilliant cast who gave this story its heart and its voice.

For Caitlin, for always being beside me.

Scene One

A corner shop, early morning.

KATIE *is sitting on the checkout counter eating her way through a bag of oranges.*

HOPE *is brushing her teeth and watering a pot of sunflowers on the counter.*

She crosses to the office to spit.

KATIE *writhes in sudden pain.*

KATIE Fuck.

HOPE *skids back in.*

HOPE What?

KATIE Fuck.

HOPE What?

KATIE I bit my tongue.

HOPE Jesus, you gave me a heart attack.

KATIE It hurts.

HOPE Give it here.

KATIE Ow.

HOPE Come on, give it here.

She takes the orange and splits a segment.

Stick your tongue out.

KATIE No.

HOPE It's an antiseptic.

KATIE Is it?

HOPE Yeah.

KATIE I don't think it is.

HOPE It is, it's good. Go on, get it out.

KATIE *sticks out her tongue.*

HOPE *dabs down the orange.*

KATIE *recoils.*

Sit still. Sit still.

KATIE You're a dickhead.

HOPE It works.

KATIE *nurses her tongue.*

HOPE *toys with the sunflowers.*

KATIE They look good.

HOPE D'you reckon?

KATIE Yeah, I reckon you'll win.

HOPE I dunno. There's a bloke at the end who's grown them eight feet tall.

KATIE Is it judged on that?

HOPE No, but it's impressive.

KATIE You're gonna knock them all sideways.

HOPE I'm gonna?

KATIE Knock them all sideways.

HOPE Is that – what's that?

KATIE You're gonna win. You're gonna blow their socks off.

HOPE You're like my nan.

KATIE Am I? That's weird.

HOPE *kisses her playfully.*

HOPE But with better boobs / and less wrinkles / and less of a boner for the fit new postman /

KATIE Stop it / oi, stop it / no, don't say boner.

HOPE Why not?

KATIE (Because) It's your nan.

HOPE Alright, erection.

KATIE She's /

HOPE What?

KATIE She's a lady. She's a lovely old lady.

HOPE Alright, lady erection.

They kiss and tussle as JO *walks in.*

Her left arm is bandaged in a soft splint.

JO Morning ladies.

HOPE Morning.

KATIE Hiya, Jo.

HOPE You alright?

JO's *eyes dart to* KATIE, *still sitting on the counter.*

JO I disinfected that last night.

KATIE How was it?

JO Horrible.

HOPE Oh shit, yeah.

JO It was horrible. It was excruciating. He wants to keep the house. He thinks he can keep the house.

KATIE Can he?

JO I don't know.

KATIE What, and her move in?

JO I don't know. I'll have to spend all the money I don't have on a dozy bloody lawyer.

HOPE I can't believe he's still there.

JO He's taken up the carpets and put down fancy fucking wood.

HOPE I wouldn't have gone.

JO I had to. To prove I could. To be a grown up, didn't I?

KATIE What d'you have to eat?

JO Lasagne.

HOPE Oh.

JO It was...really nice, actually.

KATIE D'you let on you were angry?

JO I think – no, I think I held it together.

HOPE It worked then.

JO Well.

KATIE Don't go again.

HOPE No.

KATIE You've done it now.

HOPE Yeah.

JO Yeah. I know. It's just part of me wanted to turn and leg it and part of me wanted to lie down and stay there. We had Ryan in that house.

KATIE *reaches for her hand.*

KATIE We love you.

HOPE We do.

JO Then get down off there.

KATIE swings her feet off the counter and waggles her shoes.

KATIE They're brand new, these.

HOPE They're lush.

KATIE So they won't be dirty.

JO Did you walk to work?

KATIE What?

JO Did you walk to work?

KATIE No. I biked in.

JO Did you walk your bike down an outdoor path?

KATIE Yeah /

JO Then wipe it down, Katie, there's food goes on there.

She signals to the flowers.

What – what are they?

HOPE They're sunflowers. They're sort of special sunflowers 'cause they grow... What?

JO You tell me.

HOPE They're traditional.

JO Are they? In September?

HOPE Well they're cheerful.

She appeals to **KATIE,** *who nods earnestly.*

KATIE They're perky.

HOPE I grew them on the allotment.

JO They're allergenic.

HOPE Eh?

JO They're an allergen. I've told you this, will you move them.

KATIE Flowers?

JO Yes. Flowers. Sunflowers. I told you this, I gave you that list, did you not bloody read it?

HOPE No, these are different, they're /

JO I spent – I don't have a printer and you've not replaced the ink, have you?

KATIE Sorry.

JO So I went to the library. I went to the local sodding library to print you those sheets so that Her Ladyship in management would stop panting down my neck about allergens and you didn't bloody read them.

KATIE Sorry.

HOPE I'll put them in the office.

JO Thank you.

HOPE But they're not normal sunflowers 'cause they bloom in the autumn /

KATIE Just /

HOPE Yeah. Sorry.

She picks up the flowers and goes towards the office.

JO They're lovely.

KATIE Yeah.

JO Sorry.

HOPE *exits.*

KATIE *pulls* JO *into a hug.*

KATIE Are you alright?

JO Mm.

KATIE He'll have bought that lasagne and put it in a baking tray.

JO No.

KATIE He will.

JO Well.

KATIE D'you want a reiki massage?

JO No thanks, love, not now.

KATIE *sets to work cleaning the counter.*

HOPE *swings back in and sidles towards the bag of oranges. She picks a few up.*

HOPE Right. Right watch this.

She begins to juggle, her face bunched in concentration.

KATIE Oh my God.

HOPE I cracked it last night. I had this sudden moment, this epiphany moment /

KATIE You're amazing.

HOPE Come here, I'll show you /

JO No. No, I am not mopping pulp off the floor.

She intercepts an orange with her good hand.

KATIE No, don't stop!

JO Right, listen. Listen, Katherine McCarthy. If I spend today having to make you work instead of trusting you to do it properly then you will wear /

KATIE No / no.

JO The hair net. So help me God. Now finish cleaning that counter.

JO *goes to the door and flicks the Closed sign to Open.*

HOPE *goes back to juggling.*

We're open ladies. Put –

She swipes another orange.

Put that down. And fix your hair.

HOPE *gawks at* **JO***'s aim.*

KATIE She played netball for Trafford.

HOPE Did you?

JO Goal defence.

HOPE Wow.

KATIE Yeah.

JO Yeah. Yeah we were good.

She passes the fridges.

Put those sarnies on sale, they've been sat there forever.

She goes towards the office.

HOPE Ey. Think big.

JO No.

HOPE Think big.

KATIE Go on, it does work.

HOPE Arms up.

Reluctantly, **JO** *raises her arms.*

Legs akimbo. And take a big, deep, powerful breath. And repeat after me, "I am Jo".

JO *(limply)* I'm Jo.

HOPE "And I am a positive, capable, wonderful woman."

JO I'm a positive, capable, wonderful woman.

HOPE "With no appreciation of horticulture."

JO *drops the stance.*

KATIE Did it work?

JO No, look, flip a coin for breaks, I've not done a rota. And the new boy's starting later. He's closing with you (Katie).

HOPE We don't need the new boy.

JO It's health and safety rubbish. I need two of you every shift, and you both need days off.

HOPE Why two of us?

KATIE Hope /

HOPE What?

KATIE Go on, pack it in.

HOPE I'm just asking why we need a bloke in here.

JO It's policy.

HOPE Why?

JO It's company-wide, it's every branch.

HOPE Why, what's gonna happen?

JO Will you just pipe down and do as you're told.

HOPE I just think it's bollocks, we don't need someone else.

JO I'll have you twenty-four seven, shall I?

HOPE No.

JO No. Right then.

HOPE It's just /

JO What?

HOPE It's fucking – bollocks.

JO Will you watch your mouth.

KATIE He might be nice.

HOPE Fuck off, fat chance.

KATIE It's alright, Jo. We'll be friendly, won't we. I'll show him the close.

JO Thank you. Now be good.

She exits to the office.

HOPE *turns to* **KATIE**.

HOPE Do we not work hard enough?

KATIE It wasn't her idea.

HOPE I like it just us.

KATIE We'll have to stick it out.

HOPE I bet he's a prick.

KATIE Watch it, you'll spill that, it's almost half full.

She moves as if catching a glass from **HOPE**'s *hands.*

HOPE That joke is so rubbish.

KATIE You love it.

HOPE No you love it.

KATIE Go on, brighten up. Come here.

They kiss.

Teach me the juggling.

Scene Two

A week later.

MICHAEL is sweeping the floor as KATIE pops reduced signs onto sandwiches with a sticker gun.

He watches KATIE's back.

MICHAEL You get the best jobs.

KATIE D'you wanna swap?

MICHAEL Really?

KATIE Come here.

MICHAEL Can I?

KATIE Yeah.

MICHAEL How do I / ?

KATIE Just put it on the packet and pull the trigger.

He slicks a sticker onto a sandwich and giggles.

She smiles at his strangeness.

MICHAEL It's good.

KATIE Yeah.

He keeps his back to KATIE.

He stickers another sandwich.

MICHAEL She touches you a lot. That girl from here.

KATIE What?

MICHAEL D'you mind?

KATIE She's a mate.

He turns.

MICHAEL She's always looking at you.

KATIE You must be looking at her.

MICHAEL No it's just – it's hard to miss it.

KATIE Ok.

MICHAEL I just wondered.

KATIE It's nothing.

   ...

MICHAEL I like this.

KATIE Like what?

MICHAEL I dunno. All of this. I like this too.

He raises the gun and sticks a price tag to her forehead.

KATIE *peels it off.*

KATIE One pound fifty.

MICHAEL Bargain.

KATIE Cheers.

   ...

MICHAEL D'you want a coffee?

KATIE We'll be done in a minute.

MICHAEL My kettle's broken.

KATIE Is it?

MICHAEL *exits to the office.*

In his absence, **KATIE** *shuffles the sweepings into a dustpan, tosses them into the bin and stashes the broom against the wall.*

He returns with the kettle and two mugs.

Go on then.

She pinches a packet of biscuits from the shelves and slips a pound into the till.

MICHAEL Can you do that?

She opens the packet and passes it over.

She watches as he punches a reel of paper out of the receipt printer and lays it on the counter like a miniature picnic blanket.

He takes a bite of the biscuit, lays it down on the paper and turns to make the coffees.

KATIE Do you live at home?

MICHAEL Why?

KATIE Just wondered.

MICHAEL Why?

KATIE Dunno. You've got that label on your apron. D'your mum do that?

MICHAEL No.

KATIE Oh, right.

MICHAEL I don't wanna lose it.

KATIE Yeah. Yeah.

    MICHAEL *finishes the coffees in silence.*

MICHAEL I'm moving out next year.

KATIE Are you?

MICHAEL I'm gonna do medicine.

KATIE Really?

MICHAEL Yeah.

KATIE Wow.

MICHAEL I can name all the bones in your body.

KATIE points to her nose.

Nasal bone.

She prods parts of her body.

Zygomatic. Mandible. Clavicle. Tibia. Fibula. No, I'm fibbing ya.

He gives a dorky chuckle. **KATIE** *smiles. He coughs self-consciously.*

No it is. It is the fibula.

KATIE I had my tonsils out when I was six.

MICHAEL Did you?

KATIE I wanted to keep them but they wouldn't let me.

MICHAEL You could have trapped them in amber. Or kept them in formaldehyde. Makes you hungry, that. Makes your mouth water. So you're dissecting tongues and your tummy rumbles.

KATIE That's disgusting.

MICHAEL Yeah.

KATIE Have you done that then?

MICHAEL What?

KATIE Cut up tongues.

MICHAEL Oh. Yeah, loads.

KATIE Loads?

MICHAEL And an eye once, and a knee cap. And once...

KATIE What?

MICHAEL *smirks and hands her a coffee.*

What?

MICHAEL We did...

He looks behind as if to check they're alone.

I've done a willy once.

KATIE Y – really? In school?

MICHAEL At a summer school in Nottingham.

KATIE Where's it from?

MICHAEL Cadavers. Donations. People leave them behind in wills and stuff.

KATIE Oh right. Ok.

MICHAEL Not, not just the willy, the whole – y'know, body.

KATIE *smiles.*

KATIE Ok.

A shy, gawky silence settles between them.

You must be clever.

MICHAEL Why?

KATIE Medicine. It's impressive.

MICHAEL Is it?

KATIE Yeah, you know it is. All doctors know it is, that's why half of them do it.

MICHAEL That's not why I'm doing it. I just like mending stuff.

KATIE You can't like it here much.

MICHAEL It's alright.

KATIE It's day in, day out though. Shutters up, stock up, and then all the same faces. Tinned soup Tony comes in for his dinner. Doris comes in for a Mars bar and bangs on about City 'cause she knows Jo's United. Miss Kirby comes in for twenty-four eggs every Monday morning. She teaches food tech at Loretto.

MICHAEL Right. Ok.

KATIE You'll get to know them. Nothing much changes. Apart from once when a lady slipped on a wet patch and fell with her face in a box of kiwis. She was allergic. I had to give her an EpiPen. And now Jo's all militant 'cause she got shouted at by the area manager...but that was six months ago and nothing good's happened since then.

MICHAEL *studies her quietly.*

MICHAEL You're brave, I reckon.

KATIE Nah, I've done it before. Hope's allergic to peanuts and we went to this posh hotel as a treat last Christmas and there was peanut oil in the soap or something.

Her words trail off and she laughs nervously, suddenly aware of her clumsy confession.

She stares into her coffee and blows down to cool it.

MICHAEL *reaches out and cups his hands over hers.*

MICHAEL Don't blow it like that.

KATIE What?

MICHAEL If you blow down the heat just gets rearranged.

KATIE – Ok.

MICHAEL You should blow across it.

She moves to shrug him off but he tightens his grip with a whisper of laughter.

Go on, have a go.

KATIE I can do my own coffee.

MICHAEL Here, I'll show you.

He moves towards her as she tugs away.

The coffee slops across the counter.

KATIE Shit /

MICHAEL Sorry /

He reaches for a cloth.

KATIE I'll do it /

MICHAEL S'alright.

KATIE *pulls off her apron.*

KATIE I just washed this as well.

MICHAEL Sorry.

KATIE S'alright.

MICHAEL I didn't /

KATIE It's alright, I'm just clumsy, aren't I.

He dries up the counter as she stuffs the apron into her bag.

His eyes flit from her to the counter in silence.

He gathers his nerve.

MICHAEL It's gonna rain in a minute.

KATIE Is it?

MICHAEL Ten o'clock it's s'posed to rain.

KATIE Do you – do you look that up then?

MICHAEL You cycling?

KATIE Yeah.

MICHAEL I've got a car.

KATIE Have you?

MICHAEL I lent it off my mum.

KATIE I've not got far.

MICHAEL I thought it was ages.

KATIE Did you? Why?

MICHAEL I heard you saying – that it's a long way in.

KATIE Oh right.

MICHAEL So is it?

KATIE Yeah, no it's...it is a bit, yeah. I'm just...I'm staying somewhere.

MICHAEL With that girl?

KATIE With...yeah. It's Hope. She's called Hope.

MICHAEL I'll give you a lift.

KATIE No I'm alright.

MICHAEL I don't mind.

KATIE I'm alright.

   ...

MICHAEL My mum's mate Wendy's got a daughter who's gay.

KATIE *studies him briefly, a smile playing on her lips.*

KATIE Has she?

MICHAEL So I don't mind. Y'know. The other girl.

KATIE Well, yeah, good.

A steady patter of raindrops is heard on the rooftop.

I'll get rid of this.

She takes the half-finished coffees and kettle back through to the office.

MICHAEL *looks around the shop in quiet satisfaction. He takes down a tin of soup and turns it over slowly.*

KATIE *returns. She pulls on her coat, tosses the biscuits into her bag and packs up the rest of her things.*

MICHAEL I used to have this when I was poorly. It heats you right up.

Barely listening, **KATIE** *switches the lights off one by one.*

I used to want to be ill. It was always cosy. "You need looking after" that's what Mum used to say. All like that, super strict, like an army general. And then you get tucked in and you don't have to worry.

KATIE Sounds good.

MICHAEL Yeah. Yeah it was.

The rain thickens outside.

KATIE Bloody hell. It's pissing down.

MICHAEL *bites down a smile. He sets the tin back on the shelf.*

MICHAEL I'll give you a lift.

Scene Three

Two weeks later.

MICHAEL is cleaning the fridges as JO empties the tills.

MICHAEL Have...

He clears his throat.

Um, Jo?

JO Mm?

He hesitates, then, falteringly –.

MICHAEL Um, I've not been paid yet.

JO It's...oh. What day is it?

MICHAEL Friday.

JO I'm...right. I'll – I'll get it done now.

MICHAEL S'alright.

JO I didn't do the orders.

MICHAEL It's alright, I've done them. I just put in for the same as last week plus a couple of boxes of pumpkins. Y'know, for Halloween.

JO Right. Right, thank you.

MICHAEL Sorry. I should've asked.

JO No. No, thank God, we'd be buggered otherwise.

She slips some money into an envelope and hands it to MICHAEL.

Here, take it now.

He reaches to take it and touches her wrist.

MICHAEL What happened?

JO Oh I tripped lifting stock. Bloody thing.

He keeps hold of her wrist.

MICHAEL It looks bad.

JO It's not bad, it's just a nuisance.

She pulls gently away and goes back to the till.

MICHAEL Are you alright?

JO I'm fine. I'm just old, I'm just packing up.

MICHAEL But d'you feel all right?

JO I feel – yeah, I feel fine.

MICHAEL I'm just asking.

JO I know. But you needn't worry.

He watches as she works.

MICHAEL You don't look well.

JO *abandons the till.*

JO I'm losing count here, Michael.

He nods to her wrist.

MICHAEL Did someone do that?

...

JO No.

He glances to her left hand.

MICHAEL Are you married?

JO No...get back to work.

MICHAEL Have you got kids?

JO Not – no.

MICHAEL Why not?

JO (wow) Michael.

MICHAEL What?

JO Look. I know you mean well but let's just finish up, eh?

MICHAEL Do you live on your own?

JO Get back to those fridges.

She turns back to the tills.

They work in silence for a moment.

MICHAEL Do you want to see a magic trick?

JO Not just now.

MICHAEL I've got a good one. A quick one. I learnt it last night.

She sighs.

JO Go on then.

MICHAEL Give us your tea.

She shifts it across the counter.

See, if you're poorly, there's nothing better than sugary tea.

JO I don't /

MICHAEL Listen. Watch this.

He raises a hand above the mug and forms it into a fist.

A silvery stream of sugar glitters down into the tea.

The moment seems suspended somewhere outside itself.

He hands it back.

It'll make you feel better.

Scene Four

Nine days later. Early morning.

HOPE stands up from a perfectly polished floor. She's in her own clothes – perhaps without the apron or obligatory name badge.

She picks up a clipboard and a whistle.

A line of red tape is tacked out on the floor and a cross is marked out a slight distance away.

KATIE stands at the start line in a pair of socks, a packet of crisps in one hand and a broom in the other.

She limbers up.

HOPE You ready?

KATIE Ready.

HOPE paces towards the start line and crouches at KATIE's feet.

HOPE You're ahead of the line.

KATIE I'm not.

HOPE That's cheating.

MICHAEL comes through from the office.

Is her toe on the line?

KATIE It's on the line, it's not over the line.

HOPE Get behind it then.

MICHAEL She's alright now.

KATIE It's gone to your head. You've got a whistle and a clipboard and it's gone to your head.

HOPE Right, you ready?

KATIE I'm ready.

HOPE On three, two, one –

She blows the whistle and KATIE *skids the crisp packet across the floor.*

She hops ahead of it, slipping dangerously in her socks and scrubbing furiously with the broom.

HOPE *issues a commentary –*

That's a beautiful start from Katherine McCarthy of Sale town centre. Fine wrist action, elegant swing, and she's closing in on the current world record...and she's done it, she's done it!

KATIE *coasts triumphantly into* HOPE'*s arms.*

MICHAEL *watches from a distance.*

To MICHAEL.

She's an athlete.

MICHAEL Yeah.

HOPE You're like Hercules or Paula whatsit.

KATIE Paula Radcliffe? She's a marathon runner.

HOPE She's fit though.

HOPE *tacks out a cross to mark* KATIE'*s result.*

KATIE *whips up the crisps and begins to eat.*

KATIE (*to* MICHAEL) My gran was an actual champion at curling. She played for her social club and she won like / eight trophies.

HOPE (*over*) Eight trophies. And we've never heard that story before.

KATIE I'm just saying I've got the curling gene.

MICHAEL Shall we pack up these things?

HOPE And it's a very noble sport, is curling. It's mocked like mad but it's a time-honoured art.

KATIE It's not mocked in my house.

HOPE D'you want a go, Mikey?

MICHAEL It's Michael.

HOPE D'you want a go, Michael?

MICHAEL No, you're alright.

HOPE Don't let her put you off.

MICHAEL No it's not – I'm alright.

HOPE I'll buy you a pint if you beat the marker. They don't check ID at the King's Ransom.

MICHAEL *reddens.*

MICHAEL I'm eighteen.

HOPE *measures him up.*

HOPE You an only child?

KATIE Hope.

HOPE No, I'm just asking.

KATIE You should get your nose out of people's business.

MICHAEL *(to* HOPE*)* Why d'you say that?

HOPE Don't like games. Don't like talking.

MICHAEL I just think we should clear it.

HOPE It's a Sunday, Mikey.

KATIE *(to* MICHAEL*)* She's just giddy.

HOPE What's wrong with that? I just won a book voucher for growing banging sunflowers, I get Chinese for dinner and it's my day off.

MICHAEL Why are you here then?

HOPE Just making sure everything's, y'know, ticking over. Plus you lot are lovely and giggly and cheerful.

KATIE Give it a rest.

HOPE If you stop frolicking around, Mike, you might get some work done.

KATIE She's joking, it's just she's not that funny.

She opens a bag of oranges.

To MICHAEL.

D'you want one?

MICHAEL Thanks.

HOPE *hops onto the counter behind* KATIE *and pulls her between her legs.* KATIE *shifts in slight discomfort.*

MICHAEL *takes out a marker, his eyes averted.*

D'you want to see a magic trick?

HOPE No.

KATIE *(over)* Yeah, go on.

MICHAEL When were you born?

HOPE What?

He raises his eyes to fix them on KATIE.

MICHAEL When were you born?

KATIE In August. Why?

MICHAEL What date? And what year?

HOPE 1st of August.

KATIE Yeah. 1995.

MICHAEL *writes the date on the orange skin, he blows it dry and tosses it back to* KATIE.

MICHAEL Was that a new bag today?

KATIE Yeah.

MICHAEL Just opened? Just now?

KATIE Yeah.

HOPE What are you doing?

MICHAEL Have a look inside.

> KATIE *takes out an orange and laughs with delight.*

KATIE No way! No way. Look, one dot eight dot ninety five.

HOPE What?

> *She takes out another. And another. And another.*

> *Each one is emblazoned with her date of birth.*

KATIE That's amazing. That's amazing.

HOPE Did you know that? Before? Did you write that on?

MICHAEL You don't believe in magic.

HOPE Not really, no.

KATIE She can juggle.

MICHAEL You juggle?

HOPE No, don't.

> *He takes a handful of oranges and juggles them effortlessly.*

> Yeah now he wants to play.

> KATIE *squeezes* HOPE's *hand and nudges her knee.*

KATIE You'll get there. You will. I bet it's just practice.

> MICHAEL's *eyes shift to* KATIE *and he loses momentum as the door swings open.*

JO enters as the oranges cascade to the floor.

There's a second's charged silence.

MICHAEL Sorry, Jo.

He steps towards her and crushes an orange beneath his foot.

He drops to the floor to scrape up the pulp.

HOPE *slips off the counter.*

KATIE Sorry, Jo.

HOPE Hiya, Jo.

MICHAEL This was her idea.

HOPE What?

JO Just clean it up will you.

JO exits into the office.

HOPE *(to* **MICHAEL***)* Dick.

She unsticks the red tape and chucks it in the bin.

KATIE *(to* **MICHAEL***)* Come here.

KATIE slips a packet of tissues from the shelf and stoops to help **MICHAEL**, *whose hands are sticky with pulverised fruit.*

You alright?

MICHAEL Yeah, fine.

She takes his hand and mops it down.

MICHAEL stops to watch her.

She meets his eye.

KATIE What?

MICHAEL No. Nothing.

She sets his hand down and reaches for the other.

He smiles.

Cheers.

KATIE S'alright.

Scene Five

Two days later. Evening.

The shop is vividly decorated for Halloween: an explosion of spider webs and plastic skeletons.

KATIE *strains to hang a skeleton from the top of a shelf as* **MICHAEL** *enters with a cauldron full of sweets.*

He sets it down and crosses to help her.

KATIE Thanks.

MICHAEL S'alright.

She hops down, swipes an orange from the shelf and starts snacking absent-mindedly.

KATIE They're tacky, aren't they?

MICHAEL Yeah.

KATIE Jo loves them. She's got piles of stuff, this is nothing on last year. We had gravestones and coffins and apple bobbing and all sorts. She got done by the boss for blocking the exits and obstructing the aisles.

MICHAEL I don't like Halloween.

KATIE Have you sorted a costume?

MICHAEL No. Not yet.

KATIE I'm a bloody banana. Like a wounded banana.

MICHAEL Is that – is that scary?

KATIE Not really, no. But I've got fake blood left from last year and a banana costume from my brother Sami's birthday, so.

MICHAEL Right.

KATIE It was a fruit salad theme.

She rips into another orange.

MICHAEL You hungry then?

KATIE I didn't eat breakfast. And I only had popcorn and raisins for lunch.

MICHAEL Why?

KATIE I dunno.

MICHAEL You're not fat.

KATIE What?

MICHAEL I mean you don't need to diet.

KATIE I don't – I'm not – ok.

MICHAEL Does she not make you breakfast?

KATIE D'you want a chocolate eyeball?

MICHAEL Yeah, go on.

He takes one.

KATIE It's your turn to mop.

He exits for the mop as KATIE *begins to clean down the fridges.*

MICHAEL *returns and starts on the floor. A moment passes.*

MICHAEL I could you make you breakfast one day. I love it. Best meal, I reckon. Toast and jam in the summer. Porridge at Christmas.

KATIE I don't like porridge.

MICHAEL Fruit salad then. Or pancakes. Or a fry-up. I'm good at a fry-up...or marmalade.

KATIE What?

MICHAEL I'll do you a homemade marmalade.

Barely listening, she smiles faintly and moves to wipe down the next fridge.

MICHAEL *watches, hungry for her attention.*

Is it – tomorrow – do we have to dress up?

KATIE Yeah you do. It's an actual rule.

MICHAEL Is it?

KATIE Yeah it's a company rule, and it's every holiday, not just tomorrow. It's Paddy's Day and Easter Day and Chinese New Year and everything. It's bollocks but we have to.

MICHAEL Does Jo?

KATIE Yeah, she's amazing. She was an actual anatomical heart once for Valentine's Day. She had valves and pumps and veins and everything. We got a photo and made it into cards. We sold loads last year, look, we've got them in here.

She crosses to a shelf and picks out a bright-red card.

She hands it to MICHAEL.

It goes "I heart you so much".

MICHAEL *(over)* "I heart you so much." That's good. I get it.

KATIE I did the design, all that round there.

She points to the card with quiet pride.

MICHAEL That's amazing.

KATIE Cheers.

MICHAEL No that's really good. You're like a proper artist.

KATIE I like designs and stuff. I'm tryna do it for money but I'm not making millions.

MICHAEL You've got, like – a talent.

KATIE It's Jo's outfit makes it good though.

MICHAEL *gazes at the card.*

Go on, you can keep it.

MICHAEL *flushes red and puts it gently in his pocket.*

MICHAEL Wow. Ok. Thank you.

KATIE So what about this costume? You can borrow some blood, have you got a white coat?

MICHAEL No.

KATIE Get one from Poundland, I'll do you up.

MICHAEL Right. Ok.

KATIE It's not that bad.

MICHAEL No I just – I don't like a fuss.

She reaches towards him and tweaks his hair.

KATIE And do your hair like that. Like a shaggy sort of demon doctor.

MICHAEL Are you winding me up?

She laughs and musses his hair again.

KATIE What? It looks good.

MICHAEL Alright stop it.

KATIE Come here, stop squirming.

MICHAEL Stop it.

He catches her wrist.

She laughs and pulls back but his grip is firm.

KATIE Alright! Ok, sorry.

He leans in and kisses her closely.

She pulls away.

What are you doing?

MICHAEL You're really pretty.

KATIE I didn't mean it like that. I really – I didn't.

MICHAEL You don't think you are but you are. You're beautiful actually.

KATIE Look, it's not like that.

MICHAEL Do you want a lift?

KATIE No, I'm alright, Michael.

MICHAEL I don't mind.

KATIE I'll just – I'll do the flowers and then I reckon we're finished.

She takes a water jug from the counter top and begins to top up the flower buckets.

MICHAEL *watches as she moves.*

MICHAEL D'you know what they mean?

KATIE What?

MICHAEL All those flowers.

KATIE Not – no, not really.

MICHAEL They're for innocence, daisies. And the roses are all for love, but different kinds for different colours...white means bridal, pink means gratitude, yellow means friendship... and the red carnation, that means "alas, my poor heart".

KATIE *sets down the jug.*

KATIE Don't...don't tell Hope, yeah? (about before)

    ...

MICHAEL Ok.

She catches his smile.

KATIE What?

MICHAEL I don't mind waiting.

KATIE What for?

MICHAEL For you.

KATIE Don't be stupid.

MICHAEL Why?

KATIE I told you. It's not like that.

MICHAEL We haven't tried it yet.

>   **KATIE** *takes off her apron.*

KATIE I think we're done.

> *She takes the mop.*

> Here, give that here, I'll chuck it out.

> *She exits to empty the mop water as* **MICHAEL** *takes off his apron.*

> *She comes back through with her coat and bag, opens the door and holds it for* **MICHAEL**.

> After you.

> *He goes to leave. Pauses at the door.*

MICHAEL I like you, Katie.

KATIE Go on.

> *He watches her, smiling, waiting for an answer.*

> Yeah... I like you too. I'll see you tomorrow.

> *He exits.*

> *She closes the door behind him and waits to hear him drive away.*

Scene Six

Early the next morning.

JO is sitting at the counter sorting through a stack of order forms. There's an open letter on the desk beside her that seems to tug at her attention.

She abandons the order forms and turns to pick it up.

She reads it over slowly. A moment passes.

As she reads, the shop door opens gently and MICHAEL sneaks quietly into the shop wearing a crisp white lab coat and carrying a full-sized model skeleton.

MICHAEL Happy Halloween!

JO spins to face him.

JO Jesus, you're early.

MICHAEL I bought you this.

He sets it down.

I called it Jenny. Most people think they're men but I called it Jenny.

JO – Thanks.

MICHAEL Which bone did you break?

JO What?

MICHAEL Your wrist.

JO Oh. I don't remember.

MICHAEL It'll be a carpal bone, probably the scaphoid, it's that one there.

He holds out the wrist of the skeleton and waves it limply.

Hello.

He chuckles.

JO *smiles despite herself.*

Katie said you like Halloween.

JO I do. Yeah.

MICHAEL I don't really. But Katie said she'd give me some blood. I'm a demon doctor.

JO Right.

MICHAEL What are you?

JO I'm – I'm not really.

MICHAEL Why?

JO I've not had time this year.

MICHAEL I'll do the orders if you need to make a costume. Katie said you were a heart.

JO What?

MICHAEL A heart. Last year. For Valentine's Day.

JO God, yeah, that's right. But no. No, you're alright.

He nods to the letters.

MICHAEL What's all that?

JO It's the post, love.

MICHAEL What were you reading?

JO Stick your bags in the office.

MICHAEL Do you need a hand with something?

MICHAEL *gathers up the letters before* JO *can intercept them.*

He steals a glance.

JO Michael, give me that back. There's new stock in the office, it needs bringing out here.

He relinquishes the letter.

MICHAEL Are you getting divorced?

She pockets the letter and surveys him slowly.

JO Listen. Michael. You've not been here long /

MICHAEL I like it here /

JO But I need you to know. You can't do things like that /

MICHAEL I know what it's like. If you want someone to talk to /

JO You can't go through people's things /

MICHAEL My mum and dad got divorced. But he was a nasty prick so it doesn't matter.

...

JO I'm sorry to hear that.

MICHAEL Don't tell Katie, will you?

JO Course not. No.

MICHAEL *pulls his shoulders back as if echoing his mum.*

MICHAEL You need looking after.

JO I'll be in the office.

MICHAEL Wait. I want to show you something.

He dashes to his bag and tugs out a pumpkin.

It's intricately, almost masterfully carved.

He pulls an artificial candle from his pocket, drops it into the pumpkin and presents it with a flourish.

JO How d'you do that?

MICHAEL Practice.

JO Wow.

MICHAEL I'm gonna be a surgeon. And they test you to check that you're good with your hands and good with your fingers and your eyes and all that. If I could do it already I could fix you myself.

JO I don't need fixing.

MICHAEL I'm only trying to help.

JO Well like I said. I'll be in the office.

She exits and closes the door behind her.

MICHAEL *looks after her intently.*

Scene Seven

That evening.

KATIE is sitting on the checkout counter in a dishevelled banana costume.

HOPE is sitting beside her in a bloodied white lab coat, sticking reduced signs onto a trolley full of buns. She's wearing an Einstein wig with a blue hairnet pulled across it.

HOPE He was pissed off all day. You can't be pissed off all day. And it's my fucking costume, he nicked it, not me.

KATIE I told him to wear it, it was my idea.

HOPE I told you I was Einstein.

KATIE Einstein didn't wear a lab coat.

HOPE How do you know?

KATIE He was a mathematician. He didn't work in a lab.

HOPE It's a thing though, isn't it? It's like – it's a thing.

KATIE You're pissed off too.

HOPE It's just annoying, Kate, I spent loads on this and he stole my idea.

KATIE He didn't steal your idea. And you didn't spend loads, that was five pound fifty, I bought you that.

HOPE Oh yeah.

KATIE You still owe me.

HOPE I'll give you a snog.

KATIE You're alright, I'll take the money.

HOPE It's just he sulked all day and I love Halloween.

KATIE I know you do.

HOPE And you're defending him too. Why aren't you on my side?

KATIE Course I'm on your side.

HOPE He's just – he's dead odd.

KATIE *drops her eyes and thumbs the countertop.*

KATIE I know but he's fine.

HOPE You don't have to get on with fucking everyone.

KATIE You sort of do in here. I'm not starting a fight in a tiny little matchbox.

HOPE *scans* KATIE'*s face with new understanding.*

HOPE Is that why you're hiding? 'Cause you're scared of what he'll say?

KATIE What d'you mean, hiding?

HOPE I mean playing it straight. I mean dodging me every time he's in here.

KATIE What?

HOPE No wonder he's sniffing around /

KATIE I've done nothing.

HOPE No. And you've said nothing either. He didn't know about us. The first time I told him. Y'know, said it out loud. Said she's my girlfriend. Girlfriend. Lesbian girlfriend.

KATIE You know I don't like that word.

HOPE You don't tell people, Kate. I don't get it, I don't.

KATIE I did. I did tell him... I mean I didn't not tell him, I never said you weren't – we weren't...

HOPE You can't even say it.

KATIE Don't start this now.

HOPE It took you months to tell Jo.

KATIE I said don't start.

HOPE You're too soft, Kate. You're scared. You're always smiling at him.

KATIE It's just...

HOPE What?

KATIE It's just easier like that. And I know you do it. I've seen you do it. That bloke who does deliveries looks you right up and down. And you do it. You just smile 'cause it feels fucking safer and you know that's true so don't give me all this.

HOPE That's different.

KATIE It's not different. I've seen him touching you when he doesn't have to, winking, being a dickhead.

HOPE He's barely here it doesn't count.

KATIE It's the same fucking thing. And it's not like you smack him.

HOPE He's fucking massive.

KATIE Exactly. It's not worth starting a fight.

HOPE Michael's – shit and tiny.

KATIE I don't wanna – provoke him.

HOPE Has he tried it on?

KATIE What? No, course not.

HOPE Don't lie to me Katie.

KATIE Oi, come on, back off.

HOPE I wish you'd say about us. I'm sick of being a secret.

KATIE Jo knows.

HOPE Oh great, Jo knows. But when I stay at yours we're still sneaking around. We still keep the dildos in a biscuit tin.

KATIE No one keeps dildos in a fucking – glass box.

HOPE *swipes off the Einstein wig and tosses it aside.*

HOPE You need to come out. It's not fair, this.

KATIE I know.

HOPE Just –

KATIE What?

HOPE I dunno. It's just...I'm proud of you. And I wish you were too.

> **KATIE** *feels this somewhere in the pit of her chest.*

> **HOPE** *stickers another bun or two in silence.*

> **KATIE** *kicks her foot softly. Lays her head on her shoulder.*

KATIE D'you ever wish we'd gone away? Instead of sticking round here.

HOPE Not really.

KATIE We could've done uni. We could be rich by now.

HOPE As if.

KATIE We'll be rolling in it one day. I'll do graphic design for like – Hollywood, and you can do flowers for the Queen and stuff.

HOPE Flowers for the Queen?

KATIE Yeah. Why not. You've got proper green fingers. I'm just slowing you down 'cause you're so loved up.

She picks up the hairnet and tugs it on.

Is it mainly this?

HOPE *smiles reluctantly.*

We could still go away. Even just for a bit.

...

HOPE He keeps looking at you. Whenever I see him he's looking at you.

KATIE I love you, you knobhead.

HOPE I reckon Jo should change the rota. I don't like you on
your own with him.

KATIE Is that why you were in? Last Sunday? Oi. Is it?

HOPE No. No. I was judging the curling.

KATIE Don't start thinking like that.

She takes HOPE's *hand and kisses it softly.*

They sit for a moment. HOPE's *temper softens.*

HOPE You didn't remember.

KATIE Remember what?

HOPE Two years. At the weekend.

KATIE I did! I do, but it's not until Sunday.

HOPE I can tell you forgot.

KATIE How? How can you tell? It's four days away, I can't
forget before it's happened.

HOPE Have you got me a present?

KATIE I'm not saying.

HOPE Go on.

KATIE Stop it.

HOPE Stop what?

KATIE Catching me out.

HOPE I knew it / you haven't.

KATIE I have! I have... I'll give it you now.

HOPE Really?

KATIE D'you want it?

HOPE Yeah.

KATIE Right, close your eyes.

HOPE *closes her eyes.*

HOPE Don't tickle me.

KATIE Keep them closed. Keep them closed.

She moves closer, kneels down and lifts **HOPE**'s *T-shirt from her waist.*

HOPE *cradles her head as* **KATIE** *leans towards her stomach, then presses her lips to the skin and blows a raspberry.*

HOPE *shrieks and pulls* **KATIE** *back up.*

HOPE Cheap skate.

KATIE *smiles.*

HOPE *studies her face.*

KATIE What?

...

HOPE Some lads think they can have you just because they want you.

KATIE You're bonkers.

HOPE You're bananas.

KATIE Drop it.

She kisses her.

Drop it.

HOPE Ok.

KATIE Ok?

HOPE Ok.

KATIE Come here.

They kiss again.

Scene Eight

Four days later. Evening.

KATIE is crawling slowly across the top of the shelves, dusting as she goes.

She reaches the end of a set of shelves and swings her legs off to climb down.

MICHAEL enters.

KATIE Michael.

MICHAEL Evening.

KATIE I thought you were off.

MICHAEL I thought you might need a hand.

KATIE I'm alright.

MICHAEL Ah well. I'm here now.

She climbs off the shelf and he reaches for her hand as if to help her down.

KATIE I'm ok.

MICHAEL Here, I got you a present.

He digs into his bag.

KATIE What?

MICHAEL I got you two.

He holds out a lunch box and she opens it up.

Inside is a collection of meticulously neat breakfast items – a sandwich wrapped in crisp tin foil, a carton of juice, a little packet of raisins and an orange.

She picks it up.

I picked the perfect one.

KATIE What's it for?

MICHAEL You said you don't eat breakfast. It's good for you though. You can have that in the morning.

She sets it down.

KATIE You didn't need to do that.

He proffers the orange.

MICHAEL Try it. Go on.

KATIE I'm alright for now.

MICHAEL Go on, just try it.

KATIE I've said I don't want it.

MICHAEL*'s face drops and his jaw clenches softly.*

He nods as if to calm himself and turns to the second box.

MICHAEL I got you something else.

KATIE What is it?

He passes it over carefully.

MICHAEL Open it.

She weighs it in her hands.

KATIE Is it alive?

MICHAEL No.

KATIE Is it dead?

MICHAEL Sort of.

KATIE Take it back.

He opens the box.

KATIE *stands at a distance.*

MICHAEL Come and have a look.

She stays where she is. He edges closer with the box outstretched.

KATIE Fuck.

MICHAEL It's not human.

KATIE What is it?

MICHAEL Cow.

KATIE Where d'you get that?

MICHAEL Down the butcher.

KATIE Fuck off.

MICHAEL No, really.

KATIE What's a butcher got an eye for?

MICHAEL He knows I like it. He drove me to that summer school thing and then he got me a liver and showed me inside it. And a brain, he got me a brain once. He's well nice.

KATIE Your butcher drove you?

MICHAEL Yeah.

KATIE Why?

MICHAEL I didn't have a licence.

KATIE What about your mum?

MICHAEL She – no, she can't drive.

KATIE What's she got a car for?

...

MICHAEL She can't drive anymore.

KATIE What happened?

MICHAEL Nothing.

KATIE Ok.

MICHAEL She had an accident, that's all.

   ...

KATIE Sorry. You don't have to.

MICHAEL looks down, crushed with mortification.

KATIE sits beside him. She nudges his arm.

Sorry. Show me then.

MICHAEL turns, his eyes flushed with gratitude.

He takes a small metal board and a scalpel from his bag and pulls on a pair of surgical gloves.

KATIE backs away again at the sight of the toolkit.

MICHAEL Come over here, I'll give you a lesson.

KATIE What are you doing?

MICHAEL Showing you inside it.

KATIE Put that stuff down.

He lifts the knife.

What – what if it squirts?

MICHAEL It won't. They don't if you cut the right places.

He makes an incision at the top of the eye and slices it steadily.

KATIE gags. She covers her nose.

KATIE Is that – is it treated? With that chemical stuff?

MICHAEL No, not yet.

KATIE It stinks.

MICHAEL We can do it now. You can use stuff like vodka.

He reaches for a bottle from the shelf.

KATIE Don't – no, don't do that.

MICHAEL It's a disinfectant.

KATIE Go on, put it back.

MICHAEL You did it with the biscuits.

KATIE I'm not sure about this.

MICHAEL It's alright, I know what I'm doing.

KATIE Just pack it away, I've seen it now.

MICHAEL Come and have a look. That's the cornea there. You can flip it up.

KATIE Don't flip it up.

He flips the lid of the eye.

KATIE *gags again.*

MICHAEL That bit's the iris. It's that bit there.

He signals to her eye with the tip of the scalpel.

KATIE Don't – put it down.

MICHAEL Feel that.

KATIE What is it?

MICHAEL It's the lens. Pick it out.

KATIE No, don't, come on.

MICHAEL *pops out the lens and holds it to the light.*

MICHAEL It feels like jelly. It's good this, isn't it?

KATIE I think I've had enough.

He smiles as if indulging her shyness.

He continues the dissection – slow and methodical.

They're silent for a moment.

MICHAEL Have you thought about telling her?

KATIE Who?

MICHAEL Hope. About what happened.

...

KATIE No.

MICHAEL Do you want me to tell her?

KATIE No. I told you.

He sets down the scalpel and watches it for a moment.

His fingers linger on its handle.

MICHAEL It's just – I can't really sleep or, or focus at the minute. I keep thinking about you.

KATIE Come on, mate.

MICHAEL Don't say that.

KATIE Say what?

MICHAEL Don't call me a mate.

KATIE Don't start this again.

He drums the scalpel against the counter in sharp, palpable impatience.

He rises and moves towards her.

MICHAEL Can you do me a favour? Can you kiss me again?

KATIE I never kissed you before.

MICHAEL What? Course you did.

KATIE No, you kissed me.

MICHAEL That's not what it felt like.

KATIE Don't tell her, Michael. You can't – you can't tell her.

MICHAEL Do you like that it's a secret?

KATIE I think you should go.

MICHAEL The thing is. This kiss. I sort of need you to do it.

KATIE It doesn't work like that.

MICHAEL I know, I'm not asking /

KATIE Whatever you're asking.

MICHAEL Do something. Please.

KATIE Michael. Come on.

> **MICHAEL** *rubs his eyes slowly and bows his head.*

MICHAEL Do you ever get that thing where you wish someone would touch you?

KATIE Stop it. I've told you, it's not like that.

MICHAEL It's sort of like – an agitation. But worse than that. And you sort of have to quench it.

He looks at her deeply.

I picture you. All the time. All the time.

KATIE Don't do that.

MICHAEL I can't help it.

KATIE I'll tell Jo, if I have to, you can't do this.

MICHAEL You're right, let's tell them, they both need to know.

KATIE No you can't, not Hope, just – please, just – promise.

He smiles at her as if weighing his power.

MICHAEL I'm not asking for – not – nothing big right now. I know you're not ready and we don't need to rush. But I reckon you owe me something.

KATIE Owe you for what?

MICHAEL For touching her and for making me watch and for doing all this.

KATIE Making you watch?

MICHAEL You keep /

KATIE Making you watch?

MICHAEL I was alright before.

KATIE You can't do this, Michael.

MICHAEL I was alright before /

KATIE This, this will not happen.

He thumps at his head with sudden frustration.

MICHAEL You don't know that /

KATIE No I do, I do know, and I've told you, I keep on telling you.

MICHAEL You won't even try.

KATIE No.

MICHAEL It's not /

He slams at his head again.

It's not /

KATIE Stop it now. Come on, this – this is not fair.

MICHAEL You said you liked me back.

KATIE What?

MICHAEL You were lying. Were you lying?

KATIE What? No, I mean, no.

MICHAEL We don't have to tell lies. We're better than that.

KATIE There's no you and me, Michael.

He looks at her, trying to settle himself.

MICHAEL It's alright. It's ok. I told you I'd wait.

He reaches towards her. She flinches away.

Don't – come on, don't be scared.

KATIE You're not supposed to be here.

MICHAEL Come with me. We'll go out. I can take you out for dinner.

KATIE I don't want dinner.

MICHAEL You need to eat /

KATIE I don't need anything, Michael.

MICHAEL Sorry. I'm sorry. We can slow it down a bit.

KATIE Go home.

MICHAEL I'm sorry. I've rushed it. I'm just a bit of an old romantic.

KATIE Go home, go on.

MICHAEL I'll help you with something. I'll do the flowers.

KATIE We chucked them, they were dying.

> MICHAEL *breaks into a smile.*

> *He packs up his bag with sudden decision.*

MICHAEL Ok. Wait here.

KATIE What?

MICHAEL I'll be back in a minute.

KATIE What? Where are you going?

MICHAEL I'm getting you something.

KATIE Don't – Michael, stop it.

> *He kisses her fleetingly on the cheek and slips outside, his discarded coat slung up by the door.*

> KATIE*'s breath comes in ragged shards now and she retches suddenly into the bin beside the counter.*

> *Shaking, she stands upright, wipes her mouth and steadies her breathing. She returns to the dusting, numb and holding down tears. She wipes roughly at her cheek.*

After a moment, **HOPE** *enters quietly and steals up behind her.*

She pinches her waist.

HOPE Happy anniversary.

KATIE *turns with a jolt.*

KATIE Fuck. Yeah. Yeah, you too.

HOPE *kisses her.*

She pulls up her shirt and runs her hands over her waist.

KATIE *pulls back.*

Stop it.

HOPE What?

KATIE She'll be here in a minute.

KATIE *catches sight of* **MICHAEL**'s *coat.*

HOPE What's happened?

KATIE Nothing.

HOPE You look sick.

KATIE Right, cheers.

HOPE Oi.

KATIE What?

HOPE What is it?

KATIE Stop it. Come here.

KATIE *sits on the counter and pulls* **HOPE** *towards her as* **JO** *enters unnoticed.*

I love you.

HOPE I love you too.

JO I love you too but you must get off the counter.

HOPE Hi, Jo.

KATIE Hiya, Jo.

    JO *hands them a card.*

JO Happy anniversary.

HOPE Happy stocktake.

JO Sorry.

KATIE Cheers.

HOPE Y'know, we had our first snog right there where you're standing.

KATIE Shut up.

HOPE It was my second shift, Jo. She was showing me the close and we were standing just there.

    To **KATIE.**

    And I asked you out. Remember?

KATIE Yeah. Yeah, you were a gentleman.

HOPE I'd been putting out packets of those Sun Maid raisins. And she asks me if I like them and I go, "Yeah, they're alright. But I like dates better."

KATIE *(over)* "But I like dates better." Yeah. That was rubbish.

HOPE And you didn't get it. I had to spell it out, it was well embarrassing.

JO Well it worked. Somehow.

HOPE Course it worked, look at me.

JO Come on, let's get going. You can start with the tinned stuff, I'll start on the drinks.

    KATIE *shoots a glance at* **MICHAEL***'s coat.*

KATIE Can you /

JO What?

KATIE Can you just – can you give me a minute?

JO What for?

KATIE Can I just have a second? You two start in the back, I'll come through in a minute.

JO I've done the store room, I need this lot out here.

KATIE I've got – give me five minutes.

JO Will you listen for once? We'll be done in an hour.

KATIE Right. It's just /

JO I don't need this today. I'm up to my eyeballs with lawyers and letters /

KATIE Ok. Sorry.

KATIE goes to the door and flicks the shutters closed.

HOPE groans and bends double, her hands on her stomach.

HOPE Fuck's sake, I've come on.

JO God, anything to bunk.

HOPE I'm not joking, it hurts.

KATIE No way.

HOPE Fucking timing.

She swipes a box from the shelf and heads to the office.

I'm having a tampon.

JO That's two pound forty.

HOPE I'm not paying that.

She exits.

JO I'll be broke in a minute.

> **KATIE** *smiles.*

> We'll be quick, I promise.

KATIE Yeah, ok.

> **JO** *passes her a stock form.*

> *She nods in* **HOPE**'s *direction.*

JO She's mad about you.

KATIE I don't know why.

JO What does that mean?

KATIE I don't think I deserve it.

JO Don't be daft.

KATIE It's true. I try not to tell if people ask about us. I say she's a mate if I can make them believe it. I let go of her hand if someone starts looking. It's only you that really knows, that's not brave, is it?

JO It takes time. That's ok.

> **KATIE** *nods mutely. She swallows down tears.*

> Eh. What's up?

KATIE I keep letting her down. She wants people to know about us. But if I did ever say I'd let other people down, so I'm just – I'm just stuck here.

JO Let who down?

KATIE Mum. Dad. Fucking, everyone at home.

JO Come here.

> *She hugs her closely, then sets her at arm's length and studies her face.*

> You know, when Ryan was poorly he kept on at us both to be happy when he'd gone. Not to mope around. Not to sit

in the dark. And at first when it happened I thought no, no chance, what have I got to be happy for? But eventually I got it. And in between feeling fucking hopeless I thought, at least I can be happy that I knew him. Not for long enough, but I'd known him inside out.

KATIE I know, I'm sorry /

JO You're not letting people know you. But if you did. Told your dad, and your Sami and your lovely mum and even Tony and Dorris and our lot in here. If you told them, I reckon they would love you more. Because they'd know you better.

KATIE nods quietly and quickly and brushes at her eyes.

KATIE It's just stuff…stuff happens. People get the wrong idea. People think it's alright to just – push a bit.

Suddenly, the skeleton careers into the room. **HOPE** *follows behind it.*

HOPE I found a skele in your cupboard.

JO and KATIE move apart.

JO God, Michael bought that in, I just stuck it in the back.

HOPE What for?

JO For Halloween. He said he'd called it Jenny.

HOPE turns to the skeleton.

HOPE You're looking rough, Jenny. As my dear dad would say, "You are a lanky streak of piss".

HOPE pushes Jenny the skeleton against the wall, leans into it and hoops its arms around her shoulders.

Just as she does, the door opens and **MICHAEL** *enters breathlessly with a bunch of red carnations.*

He stops short at the sight of them all.

MICHAEL What's going on?

HOPE What are you doing here?

MICHAEL Get off that.

HOPE I think she likes me, Mikey.

MICHAEL Are you making fun of me?

JO No, course not, love.

MICHAEL Put that away, it's expensive, that.

KATIE Hope.

HOPE Come off it, Mikey, we're having a laugh.

MICHAEL Don't laugh at me.

KATIE She didn't mean that.

MICHAEL Don't you fucking laugh at me.

HOPE Alright. Fucking hell.

JO Come on, take it easy.

>   **HOPE** *sneers at the flowers.*

HOPE What are they for?

KATIE Hope, leave him alone.

MICHAEL Stop teasing me.

HOPE She doesn't like that colour.

JO Listen. Michael. I'd like to have a word.

MICHAEL What about?

JO Look girls, let's forget this for now. You go on and go home. Enjoy tonight.

MICHAEL What's tonight?

KATIE It's nothing.

HOPE It's our anniversary.

KATIE Come on.

HOPE *(to* MICHAEL*)* Night night.

MICHAEL Why, where are you going?

As KATIE *moves for the door,* HOPE *reaches for her hand.*

She catches MICHAEL*'s eye and kisses her deeply.*

KATIE Let's go.

MICHAEL *thrusts the flowers at* KATIE.

MICHAEL Red carnations. Remember? "Alas my poor heart" /

HOPE *snatches them from him.*

HOPE Cheers, Mike, they're lovely.

She slings them into the bin and goes out after KATIE.

MICHAEL*'s fists clench automatically. He stares down into the bin.*

JO Michael /

He turns to JO *with new intensity.*

MICHAEL I want to tell you something.

JO Sit down /

MICHAEL It's important.

JO We need to talk /

MICHAEL I don't think Katie wants all that. I think she's frightened, that's all.

JO Right. Enough now. Sit down.

MICHAEL No, she's not like that.

JO I've warned you, Michael.

MICHAEL Am I the only one who sees it?

JO I'll pay you for the week but that's it now, enough.

MICHAEL It's not me that's done wrong, I'm trying to do the right thing.

JO You're over the line, I've told you now. You need to leave her alone.

MICHAEL No.

JO I mean it, Michael.

A smile spreads across **MICHAEL***'s eyes.*

MICHAEL We're a couple. Me and Katie. But we're keeping it quiet, y'know. It's a secret.

JO You're not a couple.

MICHAEL You don't understand.

JO She's not interested /

MICHAEL We could help you, Jo. We can help you if you're frightened or you're lonely or someone's done something to hurt you. Katie can help you and I can help you and we want to, we want to /

JO Stop it. Now.

MICHAEL *snaps his head up and looks her bluntly in the eye.*

MICHAEL You're jealous of us.

JO No.

MICHAEL It's true. You've got no one. You're jealous and you're lonely.

JO *looks at him with something like pity.*

JO You're making it up.

He rises suddenly and seizes her wrist. She winces in pain.

MICHAEL It's delicate, isn't it? It could break again so easily.

He tightens his grip and JO's *body shudders.*

They stand frozen for a moment.

He gives a hollow laugh and lowers her wrist.

I wouldn't hurt you. I'm not like that.

JO Get out. Now.

He spits out a derisive laugh, grabs his bag and heads for the door.

MICHAEL Just wait. You'll see.

He exits.

JO *stays, staring into the space left behind him.*

Scene Nine

Late that night.

The shop is in darkness.

Laughter floats into the room from outside. The door rattles.

KATIE *and* **HOPE** *stumble into the shop, laughing and kissing.*

They're drunk from wherever they've been for the night and still swigging from a bottle of vodka.

KATIE I thought your mum was out.

HOPE This'll do.

KATIE You joking?

HOPE Why not?

KATIE Jo'd kill us.

HOPE Fuck it.

KATIE Come here.

> **HOPE** *smiles and tugs a pack of cigarettes from her pocket. She gropes drunkenly at a lighter.*

> **KATIE** *tosses it aside and tugs her closer.*

Oi, come here.

They fumble with each other's clothes.

HOPE *slides her hand into* **KATIE**'s *jeans.*

They begin to have sex as **MICHAEL** *emerges quietly from the office.*

For a moment, he watches.

When KATIE *catches sight of him the piercing violation seems to stun her into tears.*

KATIE Fuck.

MICHAEL What are you doing?

HOPE Fucking hell.

MICHAEL Katie.

HOPE Why the fuck are you here?

MICHAEL Katie, what are you doing?

HOPE Will you fuck off home?

MICHAEL Does she make you do this?

HOPE Are you joking?

KATIE Michael, leave us alone.

MICHAEL What?

KATIE Please. Leave us alone.

MICHAEL You don't have to keep pretending.

KATIE I mean it. Back off.

MICHAEL Are you putting this on?

KATIE No.

MICHAEL To make her feel better?

KATIE No.

MICHAEL Because we talked about lying.

HOPE What the fuck is he saying?

MICHAEL You've been flirting with me since the second I got here.

He locks eyes with KATIE.

Let's get this out in the open.

KATIE No, don't you dare.

MICHAEL We should be honest with each other.

HOPE Be honest about what?

KATIE Don't you fucking dare.

MICHAEL I'm doing you a favour.

HOPE Be honest about what?

MICHAEL Tell her.

HOPE Katie /

KATIE No.

HOPE *(to* **MICHAEL***)* Tell me. Go on.

   ...

MICHAEL She kissed me. And she touched me. She's been doing it for weeks.

KATIE No. He did it. He did it, he did that to me.

MICHAEL Don't lie.

KATIE *(to* **HOPE***)* I love you.

MICHAEL Don't lie, stop lying.

KATIE I love you. I promise.

MICHAEL No, what about us? What – what about this?

> **MICHAEL** *slings off his bag and searches desperately inside it.*

> **KATIE** *reaches out for* **HOPE***.*

> Don't touch her. I mean it, don't (fucking) touch her.

> *Frantically,* **MICHAEL** *empties the bag across the floor and rakes through its contents.*

> *Triumphant, he raises the tattered Valentine's card.*

You gave me this. You did. Don't you remember?

KATIE What?

MICHAEL *laughs through tears of livid frustration.*

MICHAEL I heart you so much.

KATIE Jesus, no.

MICHAEL You did.

HOPE Get up.

MICHAEL She did. I'm not lying.

HOPE Get up.

He stands.

Be honest. Ok?

MICHAEL I am. I am honest.

MICHAEL *braces himself as* **HOPE** *watches him closely.*

HOPE What happened to you?

MICHAEL What?

KATIE Let's go, let's get out.

HOPE Did someone fuck you up? Or are you just a nasty cunt?

MICHAEL *utters a sharp, unsteady laugh.*

MICHAEL Careful. I mean it.

HOPE Go on. Tell us the story.

MICHAEL I said careful. Be careful.

HOPE I'm putting money on your dad.

MICHAEL Stop it.

HOPE Tell me about him.

KATIE Hope.

MICHAEL Stop it.

HOPE Go on. Who told you what a big boy looks like?

> **MICHAEL** *begins to nod with strange insistence.*

Yes? Yes what?

KATIE Hope, stop this.

HOPE Are you being a man, Mikey? Come here. Come on.

> **MICHAEL** *steps suddenly towards her and strikes her with a sickening thud across the face.*
>
> *She falls to the ground, retching with the force of the blow.*
>
> *The room is paralysed for a fleeting moment.*
>
> **MICHAEL** *turns on* **KATIE.**

KATIE It's ok. It's ok.

MICHAEL Why were you letting her touch you like that?

KATIE I don't know. I don't know.

> *He edges forward. She holds out her hands to steady the moment.*
>
> *With her eyes fixed on his, she slowly gathers his things from the floor.*

MICHAEL Don't touch that.

KATIE It's ok. I'll be careful. I'll put it all back.

> *She goes towards him and leads him to the counter.*

Come here. It's ok. Sit down, come here.

> *They sit gently at opposite ends of the counter.*
>
> **MICHAEL** *looks to* **HOPE** *and seems to wake from a daze.*

MICHAEL I'm sorry.

KATIE It's ok.

MICHAEL I'm sorry. I can fix this.

KATIE We'll fix it together.

She runs her hands across his things – his little metal tin, his books, his cutting board.

He watches.

I liked it when you showed me this.

MICHAEL I knew you would.

He reaches towards her.

We're good together, aren't we?

She smiles.

Their fingers interlace. He stares, mesmerised by the sight of their hands together.

KATIE I should have done this ages ago.

He looks at her with love as she snatches up the scalpel and drives it deep into his hand.

It ruptures the flesh and pinions his hand to the counter.

She freezes.

MICHAEL *stares woozily at his hand.*

In the silence, **HOPE** *splutters a strangled laugh.*

KATIE *moves slowly away from the counter, her eyes riveted on* **MICHAEL** *in stunned disbelief.*

(to **HOPE***)* Can you stand?

MICHAEL Wait. Don't go.

KATIE *moves quickly to* **HOPE***. She lifts her to her feet.*

KATIE It's ok.

MICHAEL Stay there.

KATIE I've got you.

MICHAEL Stay there. I want to show you something.

With his free hand he picks up the bottle of vodka. He raises it high and pours it heavily over the wound and across the counter.

KATIE Come on.

   MICHAEL *looks to* **KATIE** *with tearful laughter.*

MICHAEL Remember that lesson? It's a disinfectant.

   KATIE *and* **HOPE** *turn towards the door.*

With his good hand, **MICHAEL** *picks up* **HOPE**'s *lighter, sparks a flame and lowers it towards the glistening counter top.*

He turns to **KATIE**.

D'you want to see a magic trick?

Blackout.

PROPERTY LIST

Bag of oranges	p.1
Toothbrush	p.1
Small watering can and pot of sunflowers	p.1
Bag of oranges	p.7
Open/Closed shop sign	p.7
Broom	p.11
Labelling machine and reduced labels	p.11
Dustpan and bin	p.12
Kettle	p.12
Two mugs	p.12
Coffee	p.12
Packet of biscuits	p.13
Pound coin (**KATIE**'s pocket)	p.13
Reel of paper from till roll	p.13
Cloth for coffee	p.17
Soup tin	p.18
Envelope and money	p.20
Mug of tea	p.22
Sugar bag (small)	p.22
Clipboard and whistle	p.23
Red masking tape	p.23
Packet of crisps and broom	p.23
Bag of oranges 1.8.95	p.26
Dry erase marker	p.26
Packet of tissues	p.28
Halloween decorations	p.30
Mop and bucket	p.31
Cleaning equipment	p.31
Valentine's card	p.32
Water jug	p.34
Flower buckets	p.34
Order forms	p.36
Divorce document	p.36
Full-sized model skeleton	p.36
Pumpkin (carved)	p.38

SOUND EFFECTS

NOTES

Set in Sale, Manchester and relatively 'modern day' – this could
be now (2019) or it could be 2005. The shop seems somehow
frozen moment in time.

9 scenes, 8 scene changes – all takes place over five weeks.

VISIT THE SAMUEL FRENCH BOOKSHOP AT THE ROYAL COURT THEATRE

Browse plays and theatre books, get expert advice and enjoy a coffee

Samuel French Bookshop
Royal Court Theatre
Sloane Square
London
SW1W 8AS
020 7565 5024

Shop from thousands of titles on our website

 samuelfrench.co.uk

 samuelfrenchltd

 samuel french uk

Lightning Source UK Ltd.
Milton Keynes UK
UKHW021956170419
341193UK00005B/164/P